STECK-VAUGHN
ACHIEVE
Indiana
English/Language Arts
3

TEACHER'S GUIDE

Steck Vaughn™

HOUGHTON MIFFLIN HARCOURT
Supplemental Publishers

www.SteckVaughn.com
800-531-5015

ISBN 0-7398-9643-1

3 4 5 6 7 8 9 10 355 14 13 12 11 10 09 08

Achieve Indiana
Contents

Program Features

With **ACHIEVE Indiana,** you can . . .

- help your students succeed on the **Indiana Statewide Testing for Educational Progress-Plus** *(ISTEP+)* English/Language Arts test.

- meet the mandates of the **No Child Left Behind Act (NCLB).**

- monitor your students' **Adequate Yearly Progress (AYP)** in reading proficiency.

Begin with Modeled Instruction . . . That Matches the Indiana Standards!

- items correlated to **Indiana** English/Language Arts Standards

- instructional tips for all items that teach how to arrive at the correct answer

- **Indiana** Standards cited on every page

Have Student Take a Practice Test . . . That Simulates an *ISTEP+* Test!

- each item keyed to an **Indiana** Standard

- content and design of the *ISTEP+* English/Language Arts test

Follow Up with Additional Support . . . That Emphasizes the Indiana Standards!

- detailed answer explanations for all items—a further opportunity for instruction

- standards identified for reteaching opportunities

STANDARDS FOR *Indiana English/Language Arts*

Standard 1

Students understand the basic features of words. They see letter patterns and know how to translate them into spoken language by using phonics (an understanding of the different letters that make different sounds), syllables, and word parts (-s, -ed, -ing). They apply this knowledge to achieve fluent (smooth and clear) oral and silent reading.

2.1.1 **Phonemic Awareness.** Demonstrate an awareness of the sounds that are made by different letters by distinguishing beginning, middle, and ending sounds in words, by rhyming words, and by clearly pronouncing blends and vowel sounds.

2.1.2 **Decoding and Word Recognition.** Recognize and use knowledge of spelling patterns (such as *cut/cutting, slide/sliding*) when reading.

2.1.4 **Decoding and Word Recognition.** Clarify word meanings through the use of definition, example, restatement, or the use of contrast stated in the text. Recognize common abbreviations *(Jan., Fri.)*.

2.1.5 **Decoding and Word Recognition.** Identify and correctly use regular plural words *(mountain/mountains)* and irregular plural words *(child/children, mouse/mice)*.

2.1.7 **Vocabulary and Concept Development.** Understand and explain common synonyms (words with the same meaning) and antonyms (words with opposite meanings).

2.1.8 **Vocabulary and Concept Development.** Use knowledge of individual words to predict the meaning of unknown compound words *(lunchtime, lunchroom, daydream, raindrop)*.

2.1.9 **Vocabulary and Concept Development.** Know the meaning of simple prefixes (word parts added at the beginning of words such as *un-*) and suffixes (word parts added at the end of words such as *-ful*).

2.1.10 **Vocabulary and Concept Development.** Identify simple multiple-meaning words *(change, duck)*.

Standard 2

Students read and understand grade-level-appropriate material.

2.2.1 **Structural Features of Informational and Technical Materials.** Use titles, tables of contents, and chapter headings to locate information in text.

2.2.2 **Comprehension and Analysis of Grade-Level-Appropriate Text.** State the purpose for reading.

2.2.3 **Comprehension and Analysis of Grade-Level-Appropriate Text.** Use knowledge of the author's purpose(s) to comprehend informational text.

2.2.4 **Comprehension and Analysis of Grade-Level-Appropriate Text.** Ask and respond to questions to aid comprehension about important elements of informational texts.

2.2.5 **Comprehension and Analysis of Grade-Level-Appropriate Text.** Restate facts and details in the text to clarify and organize ideas.

2.2.6 **Comprehension and Analysis of Grade-Level-Appropriate Text.** Recognize cause-and-effect relationships in a text.

2.2.7 **Comprehension and Analysis of Grade-Level-Appropriate Text.** Interpret information from diagrams, charts, and graphs.

Standard 3   **Students read and respond to a wide variety of significant works of children's literature.**

2.3.1 **Narrative Analysis of Grade-Level-Appropriate Text.** Compare plots, settings, and characters presented by different authors.

2.3.2 **Narrative Analysis of Grade-Level-Appropriate Text.** Create different endings to stories and identify the reason and the impact of the different ending.

2.3.4 **Narrative Analysis of Grade-Level-Appropriate Text.** Identify the use of rhythm, rhyme, and alliteration (using words with repeating consonant sounds) in poetry.

Standard 4   **Students write clear sentences and paragraphs that develop a central idea. Students progress through the stages of the writing process, including prewriting, drafting, revising, and editing multiple drafts.**

2.4.1 **Organization and Focus.** Create a list of ideas for writing.

2.4.2 **Organization and Focus.** Organize related ideas together to maintain a consistent focus.

2.4.4 **Research and Technology.** Understand the purposes of various reference materials (such as a dictionary, thesaurus, or atlas).

2.4.6 **Evaluation and Revision.** Review, evaluate, and revise writing for meaning and clarity.

2.4.7 **Evaluation and Revision.** Proofread one's own writing, as well as that of others, using an editing checklist or list of rules.

2.4.8 **Evaluation and Revision.** Revise original drafts to improve sequence (the order of events) or to provide more descriptive detail.

Standard 5

Students write compositions that describe and explain familiar objects, events, and experiences. Writing demonstrates an awareness of the audience (intended reader) and purpose for writing.

2.5.1   **Write Logically-Ordered and Descriptive Experienced-Based Compositions.** Write brief narratives (stories) based on students' experiences that move through a logical sequence of events and that describe the setting, characters, objects, and events in detail.

2.5.2   **Write Compositions With Main Ideas and Supporting Details.** Write a brief description of a familiar object, person, place, or event that develops a main idea and uses details to support the main idea.

2.5.3   **Compose a Friendly Letter.** Write a friendly letter complete with the date, salutation, body, closing, and signature.

2.5.5   **Use Descriptive Language.** Use descriptive words when writing.

2.5.6   **Write for Different Audiences and Purposes.** Write for different purposes and to a specific audience or person.

Standard 6

Students write using Standard English conventions appropriate to this grade level.

2.6.1   **Handwriting.** Form letters correctly and space words and sentences properly so that writing can be read easily by another person.

2.6.2   **Sentence Structure.** Distinguish between complete and incomplete sentences.

2.6.3   **Sentence Structure.** Use the correct word order in written sentences.

2.6.4   **Grammar.** Identify and correctly write various parts of speech, including nouns and verbs.

2.6.5   **Punctuation.** Use commas in the greeting and closing of a letter and with dates and items in a series.

2.6.6   **Punctuation.** Use quotation marks correctly to show that someone is speaking.

2.6.7   **Capitalization.** Capitalize all proper nouns (names of specific people or things, such as *Mike, Indiana, Jeep*), words at the beginning of sentences and greetings, months and days of the week, and titles *(Dr., Mr., Mrs., Miss)* and initials in names.

2.6.8   **Spelling.** Spell correctly words like *was, were, says, said, who, what,* and *why,* which are used frequently but do not fit common spelling patterns.

2.6.9   **Spelling.** Spell correctly words with short and long vowel sounds *(a, e, i, o, u),* *r*-controlled vowels *(ar, er, ir, or, ur),* and consonant-blend patterns *(bl, dr, st).*

HOW TO USE *the Student Book and Teacher's Guide*

Modeled Instruction for Indiana

Achieve Indiana begins with Modeled Instruction, a section that contains a variety of practice items similar to items found on the *ISTEP+* English/Language Arts test. In this section, students will practice answering multiple-choice items and one writing activity. Following each item is a Tip that models for students an effective way to arrive at the correct answer. Also, for your easy reference, a correlation of each item to the Indiana English/Language Arts standard can be found at the bottom of the page.

You can use Modeled Instruction as independent practice and let students work individually through the items and strategies. You can also work through the section as a guided instruction activity in small groups or with the whole class. Discuss each item and how the accompanying Tip focuses the student on what the question is asking and how to arrive at the correct answer.

On pages 13–19 of this guide you will find **Answers and Explanations for Instruction** for each item in Modeled Instruction. The explanations afford an additional opportunity for instruction and are written in language you can use directly with your students. They give details about the correct and incorrect answer choices and can be utilized with individual students, as you guide small groups, or the whole class.

The first item in both the Modeled Instruction and the Practice Test is to be read aloud to the students. Directions for each item are located at the beginning of the Modeled Instruction section on page 13 and at the beginning of the Practice Test section on page 19 of the Answers and Explanations for Instruction.

Practice Test for Indiana

Beginning on page 43, *Achieve Indiana* includes a Practice Test that follow the content and design of the *ISTEP+* English/Language Arts test. The Practice Test consists of 33 multiple-choice items and one writing activity. Each multiple-choice item is followed by four options, one of which is correct. Students will answer the items in the multiple-choice component by filling in circles next to the correct answer. Students will write their response to the writing activity directly in their student books.

Answers and Explanations for Instruction for all items in the Practice Test are found on pages 19–26 of this guide. Each item is first identified by the Indiana English/Language Arts standard that it tests. Then, explanations are given for the correct and incorrect answer choices. These explanations provide an additional opportunity for individualized instruction.

Rubrics for evaluating the writing activity are included at the end of Answers and Explanations for Instruction on pages 27–30.

ADAPTING ACHIEVE INDIANA INSTRUCTION
for Use with Students with Special Needs

Every student can benefit from reviewing test-taking strategies and taking the *ISTEP+* English/Language Arts practice test. Three types of students, however, require practice tailored to their needs.

Struggling Readers, by definition, are not reading on the grade level at which they will be tested. These students commonly read at least two grade levels below the testing level. When a struggling reader reads aloud, you will undoubtedly observe the student's lack of reading fluency, difficulty sounding out grade-level words, and failure to recognize common sight words. Struggling readers often read so slowly they cannot keep track of a paragraph's or even a sentence's content. This seriously hampers their ability to comprehend what they read. Because some of these readers have no diagnosed learning disabilities, they may not receive accommodations such as more time to test or assisting devices such as dictionaries.

English Language Learners (ELLs) present a unique challenge because their levels of reading proficiency vary greatly. Some are fluent readers in their native languages and transfer these skills readily to English, but still may be puzzled by idioms and figures of speech. Others, like struggling readers, read below grade level and are still trying to master word-level comprehension.

ELLs also face unique challenges in taking tests. First, ELLs may lack the background knowledge necessary for full understanding of a passage if it relies on unfamiliar cultural experiences. Second, vocabulary and concepts common to a specific grade level might not be in place in the second language. Third, literary grammatical structures may not resemble the oral language with which they are familiar. Finally, the testing format is often unfamiliar in the home culture.

Although it is impossible to remove all testing obstacles for these students, most test items are written to avoid idioms and ambiguous language. To the extent possible, test items are written to avoid reliance on prior cultural knowledge.

Students with Specific Learning Disabilities (SLDs) usually have average or above-average intelligence but are often hindered by some level of language difficulty. Students may have trouble with semantics, phonology, syntax, or morphology; these types of difficulties are often interrelated. Students with problems in one area will likely have problems in another area. Students may struggle with input, or receptive language. They may have trouble distinguishing letters, or they may read lines repeatedly or skip lines. Other students receive language smoothly but have trouble organizing it. These students struggle with sequencing and have trouble inferring meaning from texts. Other students have memory deficits in working, short-term, or long-term memory.

Some SLDs cause output problems in spatial orientation and fine motor control, meaning that students may test well but have trouble recording answers correctly in standardized test answer booklets. Many students with SLDs must also overcome a lack of motivation and confidence as a result of years of academic struggle. They frequently rely heavily on teachers for guidance and require a great deal of positive reinforcement.

Because these students have identified disabilities, accommodations can be made for them in testing and in practicing for tests. Students' Individualized Education Plans (IEPs) identify appropriate accommodations, including more time to test, alternate forms of recording answers, and the use of assisting devices such as dictionaries and calculators.

Adapting Instruction for Students with Special Needs

Test-Taking Strategies for Students with Special Needs

The test-taking strategies on pages 11–12 of this guide are appropriate for all students, and some are particularly useful for struggling readers, ELLs, and students with SLDs. For example, underlining key words helps distractible readers target important terms and drawing pictures of abstract concepts can help auditory learners and ELLs make sense of content. Model these procedures for students and provide them ample opportunities to practice using them. However, you may need to go beyond general strategies to help your students with special needs succeed. The following suggestions are appropriate for many students with special needs.

■ Use simple sentences that avoid slang, idioms, and negative phrases as you teach these strategies. Speak slowly and pause at logical points to give students time to process and discuss what they hear. Provide written instructions to reinforce verbal instructions and define any terms that may confuse students. When possible, use graphic organizers.

■ Help students build word webs or word banks that explore and link operational words common to test items. For example, a word web for *contrast* would include words and phrases such as *difference, distinguish, tell apart, unalike,* and *compare.* In math, a word web for *add* would include *altogether, sum, plus,* and *in all.* Tell students that learning these words in groups will help them decide quickly and accurately what a test item is asking. Encourage students to look for and underline these key words in test items. This strategy is particularly helpful for ELLs.

■ Help students make a chart of common words and suffixes that identify test items such as *compare and contrast.* For example, -*er, more,*

and *less* form a group that implies comparison and contrast, as do -*est, most,* and *least.* Students should recognize that test items might not use the actual words *compare* or *contrast.*

■ Give students applied practice of tested skills. For example, show students a picture of a common, easily recognized item such as a house or a dog. Ask students to describe the object. What color is it? How big is it? What details can they list? Then show students a picture of the same object that is a different style or type. Have students compare and contrast the two objects. Have students find as many similarities and differences as possible. You may want to use a Venn diagram to record these ideas.

As students become more proficient, guide them through similar exercises involving things they know well but must recall from memory: two musicians or two movies, for example.

■ Ask students whose test-taking skills have improved to guide other students through several test items. Putting the process into their own words by teaching a peer will reinforce the process and build their confidence. Supervise the students' explanations, encouraging them and augmenting their explanations when needed.

■ Teach students to access their prior knowledge about passages they read, math problems they work, and the testing process in general. Use practice test items to lead students to recognize that the items are like many others they have completed in class or on homework.

■ Since the test format itself may intimidate some students, help them achieve a sense of ownership by using the white space on the test pages to their advantage. Reduce students' anxiety by encouraging them to mark on test items, underlining familiar terms, drawing pictures or diagrams when these are helpful, and showing their work as they eliminate incorrect responses.

■ Help students develop strategies for pacing themselves during the test period. Students with special needs can get stuck on a test item and spend too much time on it. Teach students to use a watch or clock to monitor their time.

Time management includes knowing when to skip an item and move on, returning to the skipped item if time allows. Teach students how to skip items and return to them. Students with output processing SLDs especially worry about leaving answers blank and need explicit practice in matching answers to the correct lines.

■ Teach students to break long test passages into more manageable chunks. Practice with students reading a paragraph or a few sentences and underlining key words and phrases. Have students write notes in the margins of the passage to help them remember where key information can be found.

■ A similar strategy can be used for decoding long words with prefixes and suffixes or compound words.

■ Work with students to discover the meaning of unfamiliar words and idioms from the context of the surrounding sentences.

Additional Strategies for Students with Specific Learning Disabilities

■ Review each student's IEP to learn what accommodations are permitted during testing, or ask the student's counselor to provide a list of accommodations. Use these accommodations during the practice test so the student will not be surprised during the actual test.

■ Teach behaviors that help students return to the test item by interrupting their work on the test item, then returning to the beginning of the item rather than picking up where they left off.

■ To alleviate students' anxiety, ensure that the practice test environment is as close to the actual test environment as possible. If students are allowed to record their answers orally on tape, be sure they do so during the practice test. If they are allowed to use manipulatives or assisting devices, be sure to provide them during the practice test.

■ Teach students to segment complex instructions. For example, if a test item requires an extended response that asks students first to compare and then to draw conclusions, model how to find each instruction and mark it, perhaps as "Step 1" and "Step 2." Guide students as they respond to one step at a time and encourage them to review the question after they have recorded their answer to check that part of their answer matches each step. This strategy can also help struggling readers and ELLs.

■ Model each test-taking process and strategy explicitly and repeatedly. Students with SLDs need guidance, repetition, and positive feedback as they tackle standardized testing situations.

PREPARING STUDENTS FOR *the ISTEP+ Practice Test*

Before giving the Practice Test, take some time to discuss these test-taking tips with students.

General Test-Taking Strategies

Time Use
- Don't spend too much time on any one item

- Work rapidly but comfortably

- Return to unanswered items if time permits

- Use any time remaining to review answers

- Use a clock to keep track of time

Error Avoidance
- Pay careful attention to directions

- Determine clearly what is being asked

- Mark answers in the appropriate place

- Check all answers if time permits

Reasoning
- Read the entire item or passage and all choices before answering

- Apply what has been learned

Guessing
- Answer all items on the test

- Try to eliminate known incorrect answer choices before guessing

Test-Taking Strategies for Multiple-Choice Items

The *ISTEP+* English/Language Arts test contains 33 items in multiple-choice format. Specific strategies can help students work through the multiple-choice items most effectively and efficiently. Here are some helpful strategies to discuss with students.

1. Read all directions thoroughly before answering any items. Misinterpreting directions can lead to incorrect answers.

2. Look for and underline or highlight key words as you read through the passage and item.

3. If an item seems complicated, draw a diagram or picture to represent the item. This can make abstract or confusing concepts seem easier to understand and manage.

4. If an item seems too difficult to answer, skip it and move on to other items. Later, the item may seem easier to answer. When you finish the test, go back and answer any items you skipped.

5. Make sure your marks are clear and dark and erase any mistakes as thoroughly as possible.

Test-Taking Strategies for Writing Activity

The *ISTEP+* English/Language Arts test includes one writing activity. These strategies can help students work through the writing activity effectively and efficiently. Take some time to discuss them with students.

1. Write legibly and clearly.

2. Use available space to plan your responses before you begin writing. For example, you can use the graphic organizer to help you write the beginning, middle, and end of your response.

Administering the ISTEP+ Practice Test

Be sure that each student has the following materials before testing begins:

■ The student book

■ Pencils (with erasers) for marking answers

The test should be administered in three sessions. It will take approximately 2 hours and 7 minutes of class time.

Test	Preparation Time	Testing Time
Test 1	5 minutes	30 minutes
Test 2	5 minutes	27 minutes
Test 3	5 minutes	55 minutes

Answers and Explanations for Instruction

MODELED INSTRUCTION

Test 1

(pages 4–13)

For Number 1 only, read the directions in bold and the sentence in brackets aloud to the students.

1. **Listen to this sentence.**

   [I wore my blue coat.]

   Look at the sentence. Find the word with the same beginning sound as "blue . . . blue." Fill in the circle next to the correct answer.

   ● **Correct.** *Blanket* **begins with** *bl-* **just like** *blue.*
   ○ Incorrect. *About* begins with *a-*, not *bl-* like *blue.*
   ○ Incorrect. *Clean* begins with *cl-*, not *bl-* like *blue.*
   ○ Incorrect. *Bread* begins with *br-*, not *bl-* like *blue.*

2. ○ Incorrect. To form the past tense, double the last consonant in *hop, p,* before adding *-ed.*
   ○ Incorrect. Do not add *-pied* to the end of *hop.* Add *-ped* only.
   ○ Incorrect. Do not write the vowel, *o,* twice. Write the consonant, *p,* twice.
   ● **Correct. Write** *p,* **the last consonant in** *hop,* **twice, and add** *-ed* **to the end.**

3. ○ Incorrect. Subjects that begin with *B* would be in Book 2.
   ● **Correct. This book would have information about subjects that begin with** *I.*
   ○ Incorrect. This book would give much information about subjects that start with *M,* but not *Indiana.*
   ○ Incorrect. This book would have information about subjects that begin with *T,* so information about *Indiana* would probably not be here.

4. ○ Incorrect. The subject is at the end of the sentence, and *the* needs to be placed directly before *mountains.*
   ○ Incorrect. The subject, *Andy,* is in the middle of the predicate (a verb and the words that go with it), *ran across the hall,* in this sentence.
   ● **Correct. The subject comes first, then the predicate follows it in this sentence.**
   ○ Incorrect. The predicate, *is cute,* comes before the subject, *Samuel's puppy,* in this sentence.

5. ● **Correct. This sentence has a subject and a predicate.**
   ○ Incorrect. This group of words does not make sense.
   ○ Incorrect. This group of words has a predicate, but it does not have a subject. The sentence does not tell who or what is on the phone.
   ○ Incorrect. This group of words has neither a subject nor a complete predicate.

6. ○ Incorrect. *Wat* is not spelled correctly. There should be an *h* before the vowel *a.*
   ○ Incorrect. *Watt* is a different word. It tells how bright a light is. It does not fit in this sentence.
   ● **Correct.** *What* **is spelled correctly.**
   ○ Incorrect. The letter *t* should not be written twice.

7. ○ Incorrect. Since Chapter 1 is about types of bicycles, you could not learn about fixing a bicycle tire there.
   ○ Incorrect. Since Chapter 2 is about safe places to ride, you could not learn about fixing a tire there.
   ● **Correct. Fixing a bicycle tire is one kind of bicycle repair. Since Chapter 3 is about bicycle repair, you could find out about fixing a tire there.**
   ○ Incorrect. Fixing a tire is not a rule of riding a bicycle.

8. ○ Incorrect. *Potato* follows the rule that *-es*, not just *-s*, should be added at the end to make the word plural.
   ○ Incorrect. *Potatoies* is not spelled correctly. *Potato* follows that rule that *-es*, not *-ies*, should be at the end of the plural form of the word.
   ● **Correct. *Potatoes* is spelled correctly. *Potato* follows the rule that *-es* added at the end will make this word plural.**
   ○ Incorrect. The word must be plural. *Potatoe* is an incorrectly spelled word.

9. ○ Incorrect. The word *bake* is misspelled.
   ○ Incorrect. The word *bake* is misspelled.
   ● **Correct. The *e* at the end of *bake* means the *a* in *bake* is a long vowel. *Bake* correctly tells what the mother will do to the cake.**
   ○ Incorrect. When two vowels are grouped together, as in *beak,* the first vowel, *e,* sounds like its name and is a long vowel.

10. ○ Incorrect. *Calm* is not the opposite of *together.* It is the opposite of *fierce.*
    ○ Incorrect. *Fierce* is not the opposite of *together.* It is the opposite of *calm.*
    ● **Correct. *Apart* is the opposite of *together.* It means "away from."**
    ○ Incorrect. *Safe* is not the opposite of *together.* It is the opposite of *dangerous.*

11. ○ Incorrect. There is no picture of a library on Orange Lane.
    ● **Correct. The picture of the library is on Apple Road.**
    ○ Incorrect. There is no picture of a library on Ocean Street.
    ○ Incorrect. There is no picture of a library facing Wood Avenue.

Peanut Butter Bait (pages 14–16)

12. ○ Incorrect. Grandpa Brenner might like all kinds of crawly things, but in the story Samantha says that Owen is the one who likes all kinds of crawly things.
    ○ Incorrect. Uncle Henry does show Owen his plastic worms so that he will not have to use live worms. But Samantha says that Owen is the one who likes all kinds of crawly things.
    ○ Incorrect. Samantha says that she thinks crawly things are creepy.
    ● **Correct. When Owen says that he does not want to use worms as bait, Samantha says that it is because he likes all kinds of crawly things.**

13. ○ Incorrect. Owen may or may not eat his sandwich. He may continue to use it as bait because it works so well.
    ○ Incorrect. It is possible that Owen will try to catch a larger fish, but the story is about the kinds of bait used to catch fish, not who can catch the largest fish.
    ● **Correct. Owen likes all kinds of crawly things and does not want to hurt the worms, so he will probably throw the fish back in the water.**
    ○ Incorrect. Since the peanut butter sandwich works so well, Owen probably will not change his bait. Owen has already said that he does not think the fish will like the plastic worms.

14. ● **Correct. Owen uses a piece of his sandwich as bait to catch a fish.**
    ○ Incorrect. The story does not say that Owen gives part of his sandwich to Samantha. He uses it as bait.
    ○ Incorrect. Owen does not leave his sandwich at home. He has it with him on the fishing trip and uses a piece of it to catch a fish.
    ○ Incorrect. Owen does not eat his sandwich as soon as he gets into the boat. If he had eaten his sandwich, he would not be able to use a piece of it as bait.

15. ○ Incorrect. Uncle Henry did bring plastic worms on the boat. He offered them to Owen.
    ○ Incorrect. Samantha did not use a plastic worm. She used a real worm to bait her hook.
    ● **Correct. Owen believed that the fish would not find plastic worms very tasty.**
    ○ Incorrect. Grandpa Benner asked Owen to think of something else that will work as bait.

A Writer With Imagination (pages 17–20)

16. ○ Incorrect. The story does not say whether Angela played soccer at her new school. It says books helped her feel better.
    ● **Correct. Books helped Angela adjust to being the new child at school.**
    ○ Incorrect. According to the story, Angela moved to Texas in 1975 and worked at a law office. This event happened after she was a child in school; it did not help her feel better about moving.
    ○ Incorrect. The story does not say whether Angela wrote plays when she was the new child at school.

17. ● **Correct. The author wants to give the reader information about Angela Shelf Medearis's life and her work as a children's author.**
    ○ Incorrect. The author talks about Virginia in the story but does not try to get the reader to move to Virginia.

○ Incorrect. The author says that Angela Shelf Medearis writes fairy tales, but the story does not explain the history of fairy tales.
○ Incorrect. The author does say that Angela Shelf Medearis once worked in a law office, but the reason the author wrote the story is to give information about Angela Shelf Medearis's life and her work as a children's author.

18. ○ Incorrect. Angela Shelf Medearis once worked in a law office, but the story does not say that she noticed there were few children's books about law offices.
    ○ Incorrect. Angela Shelf Medearis moved to Texas when she grew up. She did not notice that there were few children's books about the state.
    ○ Incorrect. Angela Shelf Medearis grew up in Virginia. She did not notice that there were few children's books about the history of the state.
    ● **Correct. Angela Shelf Medearis read many children's books when she was young. She always wanted to read stories about African American families, but she noticed that there were not many books on this subject.**

19. ○ Incorrect. Someone would not read this story to learn how to write a children's book. The story tells about Angela Shelf Medearis and her writing, but it does not tell how to write a children's book.
    ○ Incorrect. Someone would not read this story to read about African American families in Texas. The story only briefly mentions African Americans.
    ○ Incorrect. This story is not made up. It is also not about life in 1975. It is a true story about the life of Angela Shelf Medearis and her work as a children's author.
    ● **Correct. Someone would read this story to learn about Angela Shelf Medearis.**

20. ● **Correct. When Angela Shelf Medearis was a young girl, her teachers told her that she was a good writer.**
    ○ Incorrect. The story says that Angela Shelf Medearis loved to read, but it does not say that her teachers told her to read a certain number of books.
    ○ Incorrect. Angela Shelf Medearis already enjoyed reading books. Her teachers did not have to tell her that reading could be fun.
    ○ Incorrect. Although the story says that Angela Shelf Medearis pretended to be the star in fairy tales, it does not say that her teachers told her to do this.

21. ○ Incorrect. The story says that the only pet Angela Shelf Medearis owns is a rubber chicken. She has won prizes for writing books, not for caring for animals.
    ○ Incorrect. The story does say that Angela owns more than 500 books. It does not say that she has won prizes for owning them.
    ● **Correct. The story says that Angela Shelf Medearis has won many prizes for writing good books and being a very good storyteller.**
    ○ Incorrect. It may be true that Angela Shelf Medearis has helped people in Texas, but the story does not say that she has won any prizes for doing this.

Test 2

(pages 21–29)

1. ○ Incorrect. Mike's words should be set in quotation marks and should begin with a capital letter.
   ○ Incorrect. The *o* in *our* should be capitalized as the first letter of the first word in a sentence.

● **Correct. All of the words are correctly capitalized; the comma comes after the word *it* and before the closing quotation mark. The quotation marks are used correctly to show the words Rob said.**
   ○ Incorrect. The quotation marks should be placed around Gordon's words—before *this* and after the exclamation point; the *t* in *this* should be capitalized.

2. ○ Incorrect. Although *Junior* is commonly abbreviated, no one is born on *Junior*.
   ○ Incorrect. June and January are both months, but the *a* in *Jan.* hints that Kevin was not born in June.
   ○ Incorrect. Although *Judge* and *Jan.* both begin with the letter *J*, no one is born on *Judge*.
   ● **Correct. *Jan.* is the shortened form of *January.***

3. ● **Correct. A *newspaper* is paper that has important events, or news, written on it.**
   ○ Incorrect. Although made-up stories may be written on paper, *news* is information about real events.
   ○ Incorrect. A newspaper is filled with news; it is not blank.
   ○ Incorrect. Although *newspaper* and *new paper* sound similar, a newspaper contains news; *new paper* is paper that has never been used.

4. ● **Correct. The commas are correctly placed after the first and second items in this series.**
   ○ Incorrect. This group of words contains no commas, but it needs commas after the first and second items.
   ○ Incorrect. There should not be a comma after *and*; a comma is required after *shoes*.
   ○ Incorrect. The comma after *bushes* is correct, but another comma is required after *trees*.

5. ○ Incorrect. Since the sentence describes what Sarah did "last Saturday," the sentence requires a past tense verb, not a present tense verb.
   ● **Correct. *Went,* a past tense verb, correctly describes what Sarah did in the past, that is, "last Saturday."**
   ○ Incorrect. *Gone* cannot function as a verb without a helping verb.
   ○ Incorrect. *Will go* tells what Sarah will do in the future; however, the sentence describes what she did in the past.

6. ○ Incorrect. The weather will be sunny and hot on Sunday and Monday but not on Wednesday.
   ○ Incorrect. The weather will be cloudy and warm on Tuesday but not on Wednesday.
   ● **Correct. The weather on Wednesday will be rainy and cool.**
   ○ Incorrect. The weather will be stormy and cool on Thursday but not on Wednesday.

7. ○ Incorrect. Charlie should not write *With much love* to someone he does not know. Also, he should sign both his first and last name.
   ○ Incorrect. Charlie should not write *love* to someone he does not know. Also, he should sign both his first and last name, not just his initials.
   ● **Correct. Since Charlie does not know Mr. Travis, he should write *Very truly yours* and sign both his first and last name.**
   ○ Incorrect. Charlie should not write *Your friend* to someone he does not know. Also, he should sign both his first and last name.

8. ○ *Coins* makes sense in the first sentence but does not make sense in the second sentence.
   ● **Correct. *Change* makes sense in both sentences.**

○ Incorrect. *Buy* makes sense in the second sentence but does not make sense in the first sentence.
○ Incorrect. *Wear* makes sense in the second sentence but does not make sense in the first sentence.

9. ● **Correct. The suffix *-ful* means "full of," so *cheerful* means "full of" or "with a lot of" cheer.**
   ○ Incorrect. The suffix *-ful* means "full of," not "without." So *cheerful* does not mean "without any cheer."
   ○ Incorrect. The suffix *-ful* means "full of," not "like a." Therefore, *cheerful* does not mean "like a cheer."
   ○ Incorrect. The suffix *-ful* means "full of," not "someone who." Therefore, *cheerful* does not mean "someone who cheers."

10. ○ Incorrect. The sentence should start with the word *second.* Also, this sentence does not give a reason why volleyball is fun.
    ○ Incorrect. This sentence does give a reason why volleyball is fun, but it does not start with the word *second.*
    ● **Correct. This sentence begins with the word *second,* and it gives a reason why volleyball is fun.**
    ○ Incorrect. The sentence should start with the word *second* and should give a reason why volleyball is fun.

Elephants and Their Trunks (pages 30–33)

11. ○ Incorrect. The finger-like things in the tip of an elephant's trunk help it lift small objects, not large ones.
    ○ Incorrect. Elephants do lift small things like grasses, leaves, and fruit with their trunks, but doing this does not give them much exercise.
    ● **Correct. Elephants can move heavy objects because of the muscles in their trunks.**
    ○ Incorrect. Elephants can suck water into their trunks and blow the water out, but they cannot blow over trees with water.

12. ● **Correct. Elephants are the only animals that have trunks.**
    ○ Incorrect. Many animals other than elephants have tails.
    ○ Incorrect. Although the story describes the elephants' ears, many other animals have ears.
    ○ Incorrect. Animals other than elephants have eyes.

13. ○ Incorrect. Although the story compares the two elephants, it does not tell how fast either type of elephant can run.
    ○ Incorrect. The story focuses on the elephants' trunks; it does not mention the elephants' tails.
    ○ Incorrect. The opposite is true; the Indian elephant weighs less than the African elephant.
    ● **Correct. The story says that the African elephant has bigger ears.**

14. ○ Incorrect. This story is not a song, and there is not a song in it. A person would not read this story to enjoy a song about elephants.
    ○ Incorrect. This story does tell about elephants' trunks, but it does not tell how they got them. A person would not read it to find out how elephants got their trunks.
    ○ Incorrect. This story tells about elephants from Africa, but a person would not read it to learn about Africa.
    ● **Correct. A person would read this story to learn facts about elephants.**

15. ● **Correct. Although each kind of elephants is different, they both have trunks.**
    ○ Incorrect. Only African elephants live in Africa.
    ○ Incorrect. African elephants are larger than Indian elephants.
    ○ Incorrect. The story tells that elephants use their trunks to eat grasses, leaves, and fruit.

16. ○ Incorrect. Although the story explains how elephants use their trunks, it does not say that an elephant uses its trunk for running.
    ● **Correct. The story lists drinking as one of the ways that an elephant uses its trunk.**
    ○ Incorrect. Elephants use their trunks to perform many tasks, but not for seeing.
    ○ Incorrect. Elephants use their trunks to perform many tasks, but not for hearing.

My Best Friend (pages 34–36)

17. ○ Incorrect. A calm dog probably does not jump and knock a person down.
    ○ Incorrect. A tired dog probably does not jump and knock a person down.
    ○ Incorrect. An unhappy dog may knock someone down, but the speaker says that Rover is happy.
    ● **Correct. Rover is excited to see the speaker and that is why Rover knocks the speaker down.**

18. ○ Incorrect. *Woof* and *Rover* do not have the same ending sound, so they do not rhyme.
    ● **Correct. *Door* and *floor* have the same vowel and ending sounds, so they rhyme.**
    ○ Incorrect. *Stay* and *stand* have the same beginning, but not ending, sounds. Therefore, they do not rhyme.
    ○ Incorrect. *Glad* and *down* do not have the same ending sound, so they do not rhyme.

19. ● **Correct. When pronounced, *Sit* and *stay* share the same beginning /s/ sound.**
    ○ Incorrect. *Try* begins with a /t/ sound, and *stand* begins with a /s/ sound.
    ○ Incorrect. *See* begins with a /s/ sound, and *me* begins with an /m/ sound.
    ○ Incorrect. *Knocks* begins with an /n/ sound, and *down* begins with a /d/ sound.

Answers and Explanations for Instruction

20. ○ Incorrect. Since Rover was so excited to see the speaker before, Rover will most likely bark and jump on the speaker again, not be asleep when the speaker comes home.

○ Incorrect. Since Rover was glad to see the speaker before, Rover will most likely try to jump on the speaker again, not sit quietly.

○ Incorrect. Since Rover was glad to see the speaker before, Rover will most likely jump on the speaker, not run out the door past the speaker.

● **Correct. Since Rover was glad to see the speaker before, Rover will most likely bark and jump on the speaker again.**

Test 3

(pages 37–41)

Sample Answer:
Title: Plane Fun

My friend Sarah and I got to go inside a really old airplane. It was so great that I will never forget it. A few weekends ago, Sarah said that her dad got a ticket to a show where there were a lot of airplanes. It didn't sound very fun to me, but Sarah's dad said, "You should go. It will be more fun than you think."

When we got there I couldn't believe how many old airplanes I could see. One of the airplanes had things called propellers that looked like big fans. The airplane had one on each wing. When we went inside the plane, we saw a really long bench on each side of the plane.

Then we walked to where the pilot used to sit. It looked a lot like the inside of a car. There were buttons and switches every-where. Sarah and I both sat in the pilot's seat. We moved something that looked like a steering wheel. It was so much fun! Sarah's dad was right. The airplanes were more fun than I thought they would be. I learned so much that day, and I will never forget it.

Answers will vary. Use the rubrics on pages 27–30 to score students' responses.

PRACTICE TEST

Each item on the Practice Test is correlated to an Indiana English/Language Arts standard which appears in boldface type before the answer and explanation.

Test 1

(pages 45–52)

For Number 1 only, read the directions in bold and the sentence in brackets aloud to the students.

1. **Standard 2.1.1 Demonstrate an awareness of the sounds that are made by different letters.**
   Listen to this sentence.

   [Ray went to the store.]

   Look at the words. Find the word with the same *beginning* sound as "*store . . . store*." Fill in the circle next to the correct answer.

   ○ Incorrect. *Slow* begins with the letters *s* and *l*. *Step* begins with the letters *s* and *t*. The beginning sounds are not the same.
   ○ Incorrect. *Friend* begins with a /f/.
   ○ Incorrect. *Plant* begins with a /p/.
   ● **Correct. Both *store* and *stop* begin with the letters *s* and *t*. The beginning sounds are the same.**

2. **Standard 2.6.2 Distinguish between complete and incomplete sentences.**

- ● **Correct. The sentence is complete because it has a subject and a verb. *Kate* is the subject, and *hit* is the verb.**
- ○ Incorrect. This phrase needs a subject and a complete verb to make a complete sentence.
- ○ Incorrect. The word *when* makes this a dependent clause. It relies on another phrase to make sense.
- ○ Incorrect. A complete sentence has a subject and a verb. The sentence has a verb, *helped,* but it does not have a subject. The reader needs to know the person who or the thing that helped Justin.

3. **Standard 2.1.5 Identify and correctly use regular plural words and irregular plural words.**

- ○ Incorrect. The sentence needs a plural noun because it has a plural verb, *were. Childrens* is not the correct plural of *child.*
- ○ Incorrect. The word *child* has an irregular plural form. Adding *s* to the word *child* would be a regular plural ending. In order to mean more than one child, the form *children* must be used.
- ○ Incorrect. When *'s* is added to the end of the word, it makes the word possessive. *Child's* tells readers that something belongs to the child. It does not mean that more than one child was excited about swimming.
- ● **Correct. The sentence has a plural verb, *were,* so it needs a plural noun. The noun *child* has an irregular plural form, *children.***

4. **Standard 2.6.3 Use the correct word order in written sentences.**

- ○ Incorrect. The subject, *I,* should come first. The verb, *went,* should come second. The sentence should end with the phrase *over to Sheila's house.*
- ○ Incorrect. The sentence would make sense if the subject, *I,* came first. The verb, *dropped,* should follow. The sentence should end with the phrase *the cup.*
- ● **Correct. The sentence tells information to readers in a way that is easy to understand. The subject, *we,* comes first. It is followed by the verb *went.* The sentence ends with the phrase *to the store.***
- ○ Incorrect. The subject *The trees* should come first. The verb *were* should follow. The sentence should end with *really big.*

5. **Standard 2.6.9 Spell correctly words with short and long vowel sounds, *r*-controlled vowels, and consonant-blend patterns.**

- ○ Incorrect. The word should be spelled *farther.* There should be an *e,* not an *a,* before the final *r.*
- ● **Correct. The word *farther* is spelled correctly.**
- ○ Incorrect. The word should be spelled *farther.*
- ○ Incorrect. The word should be spelled *farther.*

Answers and Explanations for Instruction

6. **Standard 2.2.1 Use titles, tables of contents, and chapter headings to locate information in text.**
   - ○ Incorrect. Although games have rules, Chapter 1 is about party rules—that is, rules about what you may and may not do at parties.
   - ● **Correct. Games are activities that people have fun doing. Chapter 2 is about party fun, so games would most likely be talked about in this chapter.**
   - ○ Incorrect. Chapter 3 is about foods eaten at parties. Games are activities, not food items.
   - ○ Incorrect. Chapter 4 is about drinks served at parties. Games are activities, not drinks.

7. **Standard 2.1.2 Recognize and use knowledge of spelling patterns when reading.**
   - ○ Incorrect. *Slide* is the present tense form of a regular verb. In order to make a present participle from the verb, it is not necessary to double the final consonant *d* or to retain the silent *e*.
   - ○ Incorrect. To form the present participle of the verb *slide* do not double the final consonant *d* before adding the *-ing* ending. Doing that would change the sound of the vowel *i* from long to short.
   - ○ Incorrect. The final silent *e* is dropped before adding the *-ing* ending to form the present participle of the verb *slide*.
   - ● **Correct. *Sliding* is the correct spelling of the verb. The final silent *e* of *slide* is dropped, and then the *-ing* ending is added.**

8. **Standard 2.1.7 Understand and explain common synonyms and antonyms.**
   - ● **Correct. An *opposite* is something that is completely different from something else. *Clean* means "free from dirt." *Dirty* means "unclean." Marty is dirty, the opposite of clean.**
   - ○ Incorrect. Something can be both dirty and smooth at the same time. *Smooth* means "without bumps." It is not the opposite of *dirty*.

   - ○ Incorrect. Something can be both dirty and tight at the same time. *Tight* means "fitting very closely." It is the opposite of *loose*, not of *dirty*.
   - ○ Incorrect. Something can be both dirty and heavy at the same time. *Heavy* means "having a lot of weight." It does not indicate whether something is dirty or clean.

9. **Standard 2.4.4 Understand the purposes of various reference materials.**
   - ● **Correct. According to the page from the telephone book, Shiny Pot Grill is located at 789 Penny Lane.**
   - ○ Incorrect. Ray Q. Shiny lives at 1369 Tractor Road.
   - ○ Incorrect. Marie Swish lives at 967 Popcorn Road.
   - ○ Incorrect. The Seed Church is located at 3546 Pink Drive.

10. **Standard 2.4.4 Understand the purposes of various reference materials.**
    - ○ Incorrect. The map does not show the pond on Ocean Street.
    - ○ Incorrect. The map does not show Berry Lane as the location of the pond.
    - ● **Correct. The map shows the pond located on Vine Drive.**
    - ○ Incorrect. According to the map, the pond is on Vine Drive, not on Honey Street.

11. **Standard 2.6.8 Spell correctly words which are used frequently but do not fit common spelling patterns.**
    - ○ Incorrect. The word should be spelled *was*.
    - ○ Incorrect. The word should be spelled *was*. An *s* should replace the *z*.
    - ● **Correct. The word *was* is spelled correctly. There are no extra letters, no letters are missing, and the letters are in the correct order.**
    - ○ Incorrect. The word should be spelled *was*.

The Rabbit Hat (pages 52–54)

12. **Standard 2.2.5 Restate facts and details in the text to clarify and organize ideas.**

    ● **Correct. Amy and Emma think the cap looks like a rabbit because it is brown and has a round shape like a rabbit.**
    ○ Incorrect. The story does not mention a paper bag.
    ○ Incorrect. Amy and Emma use their cameras to take pictures of what they think is a rabbit, but is actually a baseball cap.
    ○ Incorrect. Amy and Emma want to collect leaves. They think a baseball cap is a rabbit.

13. **Standard 2.3.1 Compare plots, settings, and characters presented by different authors.**

    ○ Incorrect. Amy and Emma go for a hike in the woods on a Saturday. They do not go to school on the weekend.
    ○ Incorrect. The girls find a baseball cap in the woods, not at a baseball game.
    ● **Correct. The girls like nature. They go hiking in the woods.**
    ○ Incorrect. Amy and Emma are out hiking in a woods looking at nature. They are not at a playground.

14. **Standard 2.3.2 Create different endings to stories and identify the reason and the impact of the different ending.**

    ○ Incorrect. At the end of the story, Amy and Emma are having fun in the woods. They are not at a park, so they most likely will not play baseball.
    ○ Incorrect. Amy does not see a rabbit, so it is unlikely that she will tell her friends that she has. She might tell her friends that she mistook a baseball cap for a rabbit.

    ○ Incorrect. The girls are carrying packed lunches when they start on their hike. It is likely that they will eat these lunches rather than go home for lunch.
    ● **Correct. The story is about the hike that Amy and Emma go on together. The rest of the story will most likely be about the next things they see and do in the woods.**

Wind Can Do Many Things (pages 55–57)

15. **Standard 2.2.4 Ask and respond to questions to aid comprehension about important elements of informational texts.**

    ○ Incorrect. Plants can make seeds without the help of wind. The wind is useful for carrying the seeds away after the plant makes them.
    ○ Incorrect. Plants do not have the ability to pump water.
    ● **Correct. The story tells readers that wind can bring rain to help new plants grow. If there were no wind, the plants might not get rain.**
    ○ Incorrect. Without wind, plants and houses are in no danger of lifting off of the ground.

16. **Standard 2.2.6 Recognize cause-and-effect relationships in a text.**

    ○ Incorrect. According to the story, wind helps dry clothes, not make them wet.
    ○ Incorrect. Wind causes storms to form over the sea.
    ○ Incorrect. Sometimes wind can be so strong, it lifts houses off of the ground.
    ● **Correct. Wind blows on plants and causes them to drop their seeds.**

Answers and Explanations for Instruction

17. **Standard 2.2.2 State the purpose for reading.**

   ○ Incorrect. The story says that wind can dry clothes, but it says nothing about how to dry clothes.
   ● **Correct. The story is about how wind helps people and plants. It also explains the different kinds of wind. A reader would learn many facts about wind.**
   ○ Incorrect. The story is mostly about wind, not about plants. The story explains how the wind helps plants drop their seeds, but it gives no details about plant growth.
   ○ Incorrect. The story does not explain any information about kites. It tells readers to think about all the things wind can do the next time they are flying a kite.

Test 2

(pages 58–63)

1. **Standard 2.1.8 Use knowledge of individual words to predict the meaning of unknown compound words.**

   ○ Incorrect. Neither *rain* nor *drop* tells you anything about dirt, so *raindrop* does not mean "ball of dirt."
   ○ Incorrect. Neither *rain* nor *drop* tells you anything about a branch, so *raindrop* does not mean "a large branch."
   ● **Correct. You know what rain is, and you know what a drop is, so you can figure out that a *raindrop* is a bit of water.**
   ○ Incorrect. Neither *rain* nor *drop* tells you anything about a feather, so *raindrop* does not mean a "small feather."

2. **Standard 2.1.10 Identify simple multiple-meaning words.**

   ● **Correct. A duck is a bird that swims. *Duck* is also a verb that means "to dodge or avoid." The word *duck* can be used in both sentences.**
   ○ Incorrect. The verb *swing*, meaning "to try to strike a ball," can be used in the second sentence. As a noun, a swing is an inanimate object that cannot swim. Therefore, the word *swing* will not correctly complete both sentences.
   ○ Incorrect. A fish can swim in a pond, but Frank is not likely to fish so that a ball will not hit him. The word *fish* works in only one of the sentences.
   ○ Incorrect. A run is not something that swims in a pond. Frank might run to avoid being hit. The word *run* works in the second sentence only.

3. **Standard 2.1.9 Know the meaning of simple prefixes and suffixes.**

   ○ Incorrect. The prefix *un-* means "not." It does not mean "capable of doing something," so *unhappy* does not mean "able to be happy."
   ○ Incorrect. The prefix *un-* means "not." It does not mean "very," so *unhappy* does not mean "very happy."
   ● **Correct. The prefix *un-* means "not," so *unhappy* means "not happy."**
   ○ Incorrect. The prefix *un-* means "not." It means nearly the opposite of "with," so *unhappy* does not mean "with happiness."

4. **Standard 2.5.3 Write a friendly letter complete with the date, salutation, body, closing, and signature.**

   ○ Incorrect. *Dear Nicky* is a greeting for a friendly letter. This letter already has a greeting, *Dear Marshall.*

   ● **Correct. *Your Friend, Nicky* is a closing and signature indicating that Nicky is the person who has written this letter to Marshall.**

   ○ Incorrect. The closing and signature *From Marshall* would indicate that Marshall has written this letter. This is unlikely, since the letter is addressed to Marshall.

   ○ Incorrect. *Dear Uncle Ralph* would be a greeting. A closing and signature are needed at the end of a friendly letter. Also, Uncle Ralph is mentioned by name in the letter and is not likely to be the person who has written the letter.

5. **Standard 2.6.4 Identify and correctly write various parts of speech, including nouns and verbs.**

   ● **Correct. The word *her* is a pronoun in the objective case. It is the object of the preposition *for*.**

   ○ Incorrect. *We* is a subject pronoun. The preposition *for* must have as its object an object pronoun.

   ○ Incorrect. The preposition *for* requires an object pronoun. *Them* is the objective form of the pronoun *they*.

   ○ Incorrect. *He* can be the subject of a sentence but not the object of a preposition.

6. **Standard 2.6.6 Use quotation marks correctly to show that someone is speaking.**

   Standard 2.6.7 Capitalize all proper nouns, words at the beginning of sentences and greetings, months and days of the week, and titles and initials in names.

   ● **Correct. All of the correct words are capitalized, and the quotation marks are correctly set around Jake's mom's words.**

   ○ Incorrect. A comma should come after the word *York,* and a quotation mark should come after the comma. There should be no quotation mark after the words *said Leah* or after the period.

   ○ Incorrect. A quotation mark should come after the comma that follows the word *sleep,* and another quotation mark should come immediately before the word *it*.

   ○ Incorrect. Capitalize *Mr. Rivera* as a proper noun.

7. **Standard 2.2.7 Interpret information from diagrams, charts, and graphs.**

   ○ Incorrect. Monday's weather will be rainy and warm. The weather on Tuesday will be sunny and hot.

   ● **Correct. According to the chart, the weather on Tuesday will be sunny and hot.**

   ○ Incorrect. The weather on Tuesday will be sunny and hot, not cloudy and cool.

   ○ Incorrect. The weather on Tuesday will be sunny and hot, not stormy and cool.

8. **Standard 2.6.5 Use commas in the greeting and closure of a letter and with dates and items in a series.**

   ○ Incorrect. There should be a comma after the number *23*.

   ● **Correct. The comma after the number *23* is in the correct place.**

○ Incorrect. There should not be a comma after the word *October*. There should be a comma after the number *23*.

○ Incorrect. The comma after the number *23* is in the correct place. There should not be a comma after the word *October*.

9. **Standard 2.4.6 Review, evaluate, and revise writing for meaning and clarity.**

Standard 2.4.8 Revise original drafts to improve sequence or to provide more descriptive detail.

○ Incorrect. The paragraph gives reasons that the narrator likes having his or her hair cut. If the narrator's hair looks good when it is longer, it is not likely that he or she would like having it cut.

○ Incorrect. This sentence may be true, but it is not a reason for wanting to have one's hair cut.

● **Correct. This sentence gives a reason that the narrator likes getting his or her hair cut.**

○ Incorrect. This sentence does not give a reason that the narrator likes getting his or her hair cut. It gives a reason that the narrator would not want to get his or her hair cut.

10. **Standard 2.1.4 Recognize common abbreviations.**

○ Incorrect. *Dr.* does not stand for *driver*.

● **Correct. *Dr.* stands for *doctor*.**

○ Incorrect. *Dr.* does not stand for *dancer*.

○ Incorrect. *Dr.* does not stand for *daughter*.

Babe Didrikson Zaharias (pages 64–66)

11. **Standard 2.2.6 Recognize cause-and-effect relationships in a text.**

○ Incorrect. The story does not say anything about how old Babe Didrikson Zaharias looked.

● **Correct. The story says that Babe Didrikson Zaharias hit a lot of home runs, just like Babe Ruth.**

○ Incorrect. The story does say that Babe Didrikson Zaharias won gold medals at the Olympics, but that is not how the story says she got the name *Babe*.

○ Incorrect. The story does not mention how she felt about her real name.

12. **Standard 2.2.3 Use knowledge of the author's purpose(s) to comprehend informational text.**

● **Correct. The author wants to give the reader information about Babe Didrikson Zaharias.**

○ Incorrect. The story mentions Babe Ruth, but the author wants to give information about Babe Didrikson Zaharias, not Babe Ruth.

○ Incorrect. Babe Didrikson Zaharias did play baseball in the story, but the author is not trying to persuade the reader to play that game.

○ Incorrect. Babe Didrikson Zaharias did play basketball in the story, but the author is not trying to explain the rules of that game.

13. **Standard 2.2.4 Ask and respond to questions to aid comprehension about important elements of informational texts.**

○ Incorrect. Babe Didrikson Zaharias did go to the Olympics, but the story is mainly about the many different athletic accomplishments for which she is remembered.

○ Incorrect. The story mentions the prizes that Babe won, but the main idea of the story is that Babe will be remembered for being a great all-around athlete.

○ Incorrect. The story says that Babe Didrikson Zaharias hit many long home runs, but it describes her many other impressive athletic feats as well.

● **Correct. The story shows that Babe Didrikson Zaharias was a great athlete who succeeded in many sports and will be remembered for all of her athletic abilities.**

14. **Standard 2.3.4 Identify the use of rhythm, rhyme, and alliteration in poetry.**

   ○ Incorrect. *Plate* and *fence* do not have the same vowel and end sound, so they do not rhyme.
   ○ Incorrect. *Roar* and *understood* do not have the same vowel and end sound, so they do not rhyme.
   ○ Incorrect. *Babe* and *good* do not have the same vowel and end sound, so they do not rhyme.
   ● **Correct. *Swing* and *sing* have the same vowel and end sound, so they rhyme.**

15. **Standard 2.2.5 Restate facts and details in the text to clarify and organize ideas.**

   ○ Incorrect. The crowd, not the team, lets out a roar.
   ● **Correct. The team begins to sing when Babe hits the ball over the fence.**
   ○ Incorrect. Babe steps up to the plate before she hits the ball over the fence.
   ○ Incorrect. The ball is what sails over the fence, not the team.

16. **Standard 2.3.4 Identify the use of rhythm, rhyme, and alliteration in poetry.**

   ○ Incorrect. *Ball* and *fence* do not have the same beginning sound. They are not an example of alliteration.
   ● **Correct. *Sailed* and *sing* have the same beginning sound, *s*, so they show alliteration.**
   ○ Incorrect. Two words show alliteration when they have the same beginning sound. *Over* and *team* do not have the same beginning sound.
   ○ Incorrect. The initial consonant sounds of *and* and *began* are not the same, so they do not show alliteration.

Test 3

(pages 73–77)

Sample Answer:
Title: Flying with Dad

One day my sister and my mom went to a boat show. The people who ran the boat show decided that Girl Scouts, Boy Scouts, and their leaders could get in free to the show. My sister was a Girl Scout, and my mom was a Girl Scout leader. They both got in free.

I was too young to be a Boy Scout, so I could not get in free. My dad said that the tickets for the show were too expensive to buy. I was very sad that day.

I always did things with my big sister and my mom. I didn't know what I was going to do all day while they were at the show. But my dad saw that I was sad, and he said we could do something together.

He told me to put on my jacket and we could do something really fun. When I had put my jacket on, he showed me the model airplane that he had been building.

He showed me how to make the plane go up and down, and side-to-side. We took it out to a field, and he made it take off. It was really loud on the ground, but when it got in the air I couldn't hear it.

My dad let me try to control it. I almost made the plane crash. It was really hard to control!

I had so much fun that I forgot all about my mom and sister being at the boat show. I thanked my dad for helping me have such a good day.

Answers will vary. Use the rubrics on pages 27–30 to score students' responses.

Answers and Explanations for Instruction

Scoring Rubrics

Scoring your students' responses to the writing activity question on Modeled Instruction and the Practice Test involves the use of two rubrics that rate students' mastery of the specific writing and language skills standards.

Use the following rubrics to determine correct responses to the writing activity question:

Modeled Instruction	
Writing Applications Rubric	pages 37–41 (Test 3)
Language Conventions Rubric	pages 37–41 (Test 3)
Practice Test	
Writing Applications Rubric	pages 73–77 (Test 3)
Language Conventions Rubric	pages 73–77 (Test 3)

Writing Applications Overview

Grades 3-5

Overview of the Writing Applications Rubric

The Writing Applications Rubric summarizes the requirements for each of the six score levels. Read across the rows to determine a specific score point's criteria.

Score Level	Ideas and Content Is the writing sample	Organization Is the writing sample	Style Is the writing sample
6	• fully focused? • thorough, with complete ideas?	• clearly in order?	• especially strong in word usage? • fluent and easy to read? • very aware of its audience?
5	• focused? • nearly complete, with many relevant ideas?	• clearly in order?	• more than adequate in word usage? • fluent and easy to read? • aware of its audience?
4	• mostly focused? • sufficiently complete, with some relevant ideas?	• in order?	• adequate in word usage? • readable? • sufficiently aware of its audience?
3	• somewhat focused? • somewhat complete, with some relevant ideas?	• somewhat in order?	• minimal in word usage? • mostly readable? • insufficiently aware of its audience?
2	• less than minimally focused? • less than complete, with few relevant ideas?	• in little order?	• less than minimal in word usage? • difficult to read? • insufficiently aware of its audience?
1	• poorly focused? • incomplete, with almost no relevant ideas?	• in little or no order?	• less than minimal in word usage? • difficult to read? • insufficiently, or not at all, aware of its audience?

Scoring Rubrics

Writing Applications Rubric

Grades 3–5

SCORE POINT 6
Ideas and Content

The writing sample fully accomplishes the assigned task by focusing on the topic and presenting main ideas and details to support them. It is able to avoid rambling or repetitive sentences, and includes complete ideas by exploring many aspects of the topic.

Organization

The writing sample's ideas are clearly in order, logically developed, with the main ideas and supporting details in sequence. It has a beginning, middle and end and progresses in a way that enhances meaning.

Style

The writing sample has exceptional word usage shown through the controlled use of challenging vocabulary words. The vocabulary is used to make precise, detailed explanations, rich descriptions, and clear, vivid actions. Exceptional writing techniques are shown through fluent writing. Varied sentence patterns, complex sentences too, are included. The writer's techniques like imagery/dialogue or humor/suspense are demonstrated.

Voice

The writing sample shows especially strong mastery of word usage. It uses dynamic words, rich details, and lucid descriptions to make its point. It shows a thorough ability to learn and apply challenging vocabulary. The writing is easy to read and has a natural tone, using a variety of sentence patterns. The writing conveys a keen sense of audience, and the perspective is original and interesting.

Language Conventions Rubric

Grades 3–5

Score 4	A good command of language skills is shown in the writing sample.
	A Score Point 4 paper will have infrequent errors that are of the first-draft kind; overall communication is only slightly affected. The flow of communication will not be impaired.

Words have very few or no
- capitalization errors
- spelling errors

Sentences have very few or no
- punctuation errors
- grammar or word usage errors

Writing has very few or no
- paragraphing errors
- run-on sentences or sentence fragments

Score 3	An adequate command of language skills is shown in the writing sample.
	A Score Point 3 paper will have occasional errors, but these errors will not seriously impair the writer's meaning or flow of communication.

Words have occasional
- capitalization errors
- spelling errors

Sentences have occasional
- punctuation errors
- grammar or word usage errors

Writing has occasional
- paragraphing errors
- run-on sentences or sentence fragments

Score 2	A minimal command of language skills is shown in the writing sample.
	A Score Point 2 paper will have frequent errors that force the reader to stop and reread sections of the text. Communication will be impaired, but if the reader tries, he or she will be able to understand the writer's message.

Words have frequent
- capitalization errors
- spelling errors

Sentences have frequent
- punctuation errors
- grammar or word usage errors

Writing has frequent
- paragraphing errors or no paragraphing at all
- run-on sentences or sentence fragments

Score 1	A less than minimal command of language skills is shown in the writing sample.
	A Score Point 1 paper will have numerous errors of a wide variety that prevent the reader from understanding the writer's message.

Words have many
- capitalization errors
- spelling errors

Sentences have many
- punctuation errors
- grammar or word usage errors

Writing has many
- paragraphing errors
- run-on sentences or sentence fragments